Contents

What is biotechnology?
2

Living factories
4

Bread, biscuits and beer
6

More about beer
8

Making cheese
10

Waste water
12

Natural cycles
14

Fuel
16

Energy from microbes
18

Food from microbes
20

New foods
22

Waste disposal and mining
24

Reprogramming microbes
26

Enzymes – builders and breakers
28

Enzymes in industry
30

Wonder drugs and wonder microbes
32

What is Biotechnology?

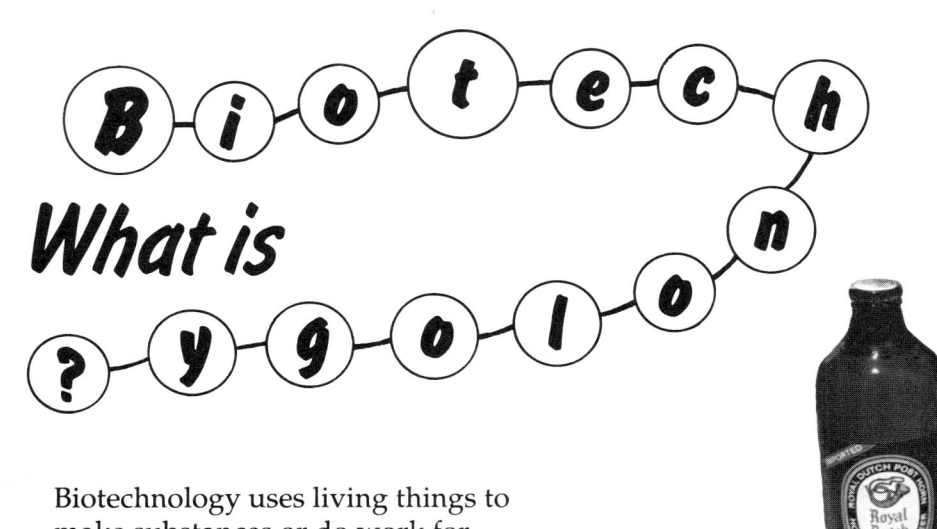

Biotechnology uses living things to make substances or do work for people. It needs living cells. Cells are always very small. They often live in groups, making up the tissues of larger organisms.

Some living things are made up of only one cell (or a few in a group). They are called **microbes**. They can be studied in detail using a microscope.

Some products of biotechnology

```
                ALL LIVING THINGS
                /       |       \
           PLANTS    MICROBES    ANIMALS
```

The microbes group can be divided into three groups of its own

```
      BACTERIA          FUNGI          BLUE-GREEN ALGAE
```

Bacteria are very tiny. They are difficult to see even with a microscope. If bacteria are grown on food jelly they form clumps. You can see these with your naked eye. We call these clumps COLONIES.

There are many different sorts of fungus. They vary from hairy moulds on bread and fruit to toadstools and mushrooms. YEAST is a single celled fungus. Fungi can also be grown on food jelly.

These are found in ponds and lochs and they make water look green. They are usually very small but they can grow in long strands. You can scoop these out of the water.

More about microbes

Bacteria

When bacteria are magnified 1000 times we can see that they can be different shapes. Most bacteria that are useful to us are rod shaped or round. For example, *Lactobacillus* is rod shaped and lives in milk. *Streptococcus* is spherical like a ball and is found in yogurt.

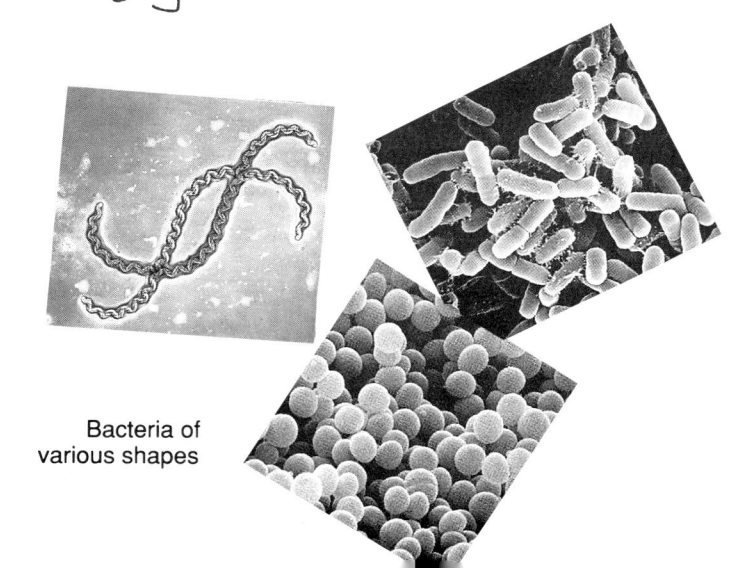

Bacteria of various shapes

Spores forming in a fungus

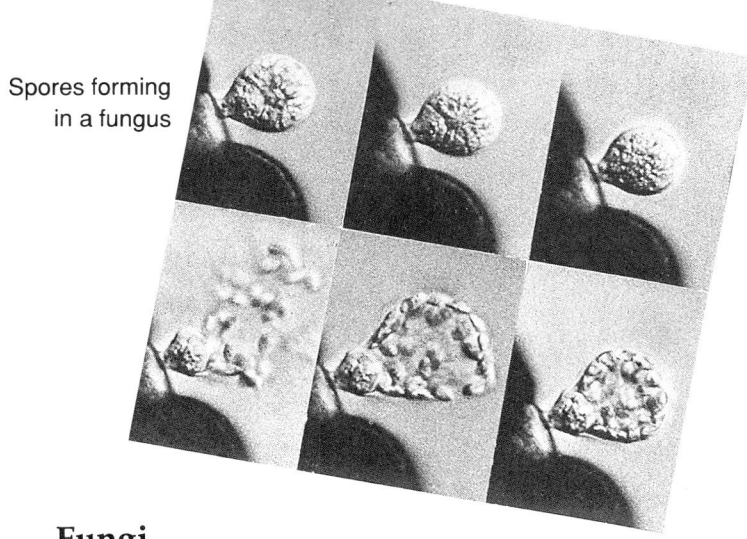

A blue-green alga

Fungi

Microbes are usually small, but fungi can be made of lots of cells. They include
a yeasts – single celled
b moulds – long branching strands
c mushrooms and toadstools – large, umbrella shaped.

Blue-green algae

These are important in biotechnology because they can use the nitrogen in air to make food. No animals and only a few plants can do this. Plants usually obtain nitrogen from nitrates via the soil.

DID YOU KNOW?

Melting microbes

The Japanese are experimenting with a novel way of getting rid of snow – melting it with microbes! Toyama, in North-western Japan, has put a network of pipes underneath a 120 metre stretch of pavement. Water is heated to 69 °C by microbes. It then passes through the pipes, keeping the pavement above freezing point. The microbes multiply in a fermenting mixture of rice and sawdust in a tank. One batch of the mixture keeps producing heat for about two weeks!

The system is called Bioheat and has also been installed under a large car park. It kept the car park clear of snow during a snowfall of more than 2 metres of snow. Bioheat is cheaper than other methods of getting rid of snow. The system also works for 24 hours a day.

DID YOU KNOW?

BACTERIA JOIN THE CID

The Metropolitan Police has solved the problem of faint fingerprints. Bacteria can make fingerprints easier to see. The microbes are pasted over the faint fingerprints in a nutrient gel. They then multiply and form colonies on the print ridges. After this, the fingerprint becomes clear.

Bacteria can now help the police to find criminals who once left fingerprints that were too faint to identify them

NOW TRY THESE!

1 What are the seven characteristics of living organisms? Which one lets the microbes release heat energy to melt snow?
2 The microbes are able to grow in a mixture of rice and sawdust. Which class of food in the mixture is the main energy source?
3 Suggest why the microbes can no longer melt the snow after two weeks.
4 What do you understand by the term 'nutrient gel'?

LIVING FACTORIES

Biotechnology was first used in the food industry. For example, in baking and brewing, yeast feeds on sugar and makes ethanol (alcohol) and carbon dioxide as waste products.

Ancient biotechnology

Bloom on grapes

A close look at yeast

There are many different varieties of yeasts in nature. They grow wherever there is suitable food. For example, some kinds live on grape skins. They form a very thin, white film (a 'bloom') which you can rub off with your finger. The first wines were made by simply leaving these wild yeasts to feed on the grapes. People soon discovered that they could breed special kinds (strains) of yeast which did the job better. Today, these strains are added to the grapes at a particular time designed to give the best results. Many strains are gown and sold for use in brewing, baking and whisky and wine making. When yeast is given food, the cells grow and multiply like this:

Yeast budding

0.007 mm — thin wall, nucleus, cytoplasm, large central vacuole

single yeast plant — budding — chain of cells

Yeast does not need oxygen to survive. In fact, it grows more slowly and makes less ethanol if oxygen is given to it. When there is a suitable temperature, a food supply and water, budding goes on rapidly. Chains of cells appear. In less favourable conditions the cells form **spores** which can survive low temperatures and drought. Yeast can be stored in dry conditions for long periods and still stay alive. This is why we can buy 'packet' yeast in shops.

When feeding, yeast secretes enzymes which digest the sugar in fruit juices. In the absence of oxygen, ethanol is made as a waste product. In the presence of oxygen, all the sugar is changed into carbon dioxide and water. Energy is released during this process:

absence of oxygen: **glucose** (sugar) ⟶ **ethanol + carbon dioxide**

presence of oxygen: **glucose + oxygen** ⟶ **carbon dioxide + water**

The result of reproduction in yeast

NOW TRY THESE!

1 The apparatus shown opposite was set up and left for 24 hours at 35 °C. A second apparatus just like it was set up, but this one had boiled, cooled yeast in it. This was also left for 24 hours at 35 °C. After 24 hours, the lime water in the first apparatus went milky, but the lime water in the second apparatus stayed clear.

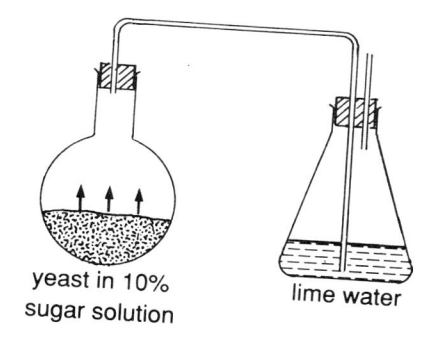

   a What made the lime water turn milky?
   b Why was sugar added to the flask?
   c Why was boiled yeast added to the second apparatus?
   d What would you expect to smell in the flask after one week?

2 Three sets of apparatus A, B, and C were set up as shown opposite. They each contained a different carbohydrate. A contained glucose, B contained sucrose and C contained starch. They were left at 35 °C. The average number of bubbles at point X per minute was counted.

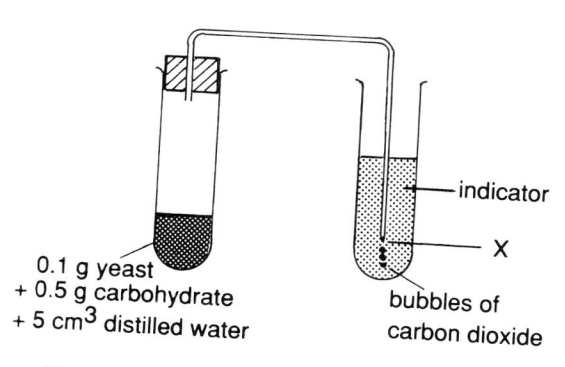

These were the results:

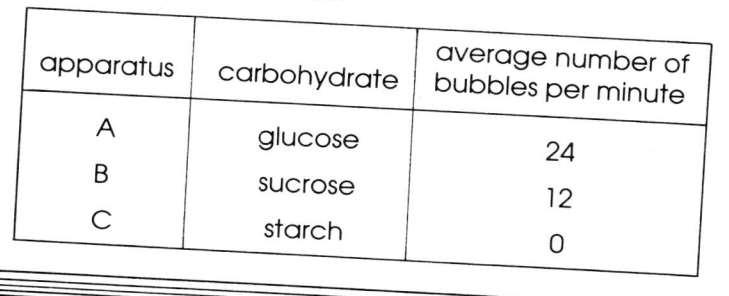

apparatus	carbohydrate	average number of bubbles per minute
A	glucose	24
B	sucrose	12
C	starch	0

   a Name the process taking place in apparatus A and apparatus B.
   b Which carbohydrate is most easily broken down by yeast? What made you choose this one?
   c When the temperature was raised to 60 °C, no bubbles were given off at point X in apparatus A, B, or C. Why not?

Our daily bread

Enzymes and baking

Dough consists of flour, water, yeast, salt and sugar. As soon as dough is prepared, the yeast starts to feed on the sugar. The sugar is changed into ethanol and carbon dioxide. This makes the bread rise. At first, this happens whether sugar has been added or not, because of the sugar already in the flour. When this sugar has been used up, the fermentation stops unless more sugar is added. Flour from European wheat normally contains enough enzymes to break starch down into sugar. There is no need to add any more sugar. However, flour from grain grown in hot dry climates has lower concentrations of enzymes. More sugar or enzymes must be added. Biotechnologists use a fungus to produce the enzymes which they then add to dough.

There are two advantages of using enzymes instead of sugar:

1 You can keep the enzyme content in the flour constant.
2 The enzymes will form sugar gradually. The amount of sugar can be controlled for the exact demands of the yeast.

In bakeries, bread is made as shown overleaf.

Like all living things, the cells in cereal crops contain **enzymes**. The grain stores starch. We grind this to make flour. Inside the grain there are various enzymes which break starch down into sugar. The sugar can be broken down further by enzymes in yeast.

Bread, biscuits and beer

How bread is made

1 A 'sponge' or starting mixture is made which contains only part of the total amount of flour. This is kneaded in a mixer for several minutes. It is then fermented for several hours.

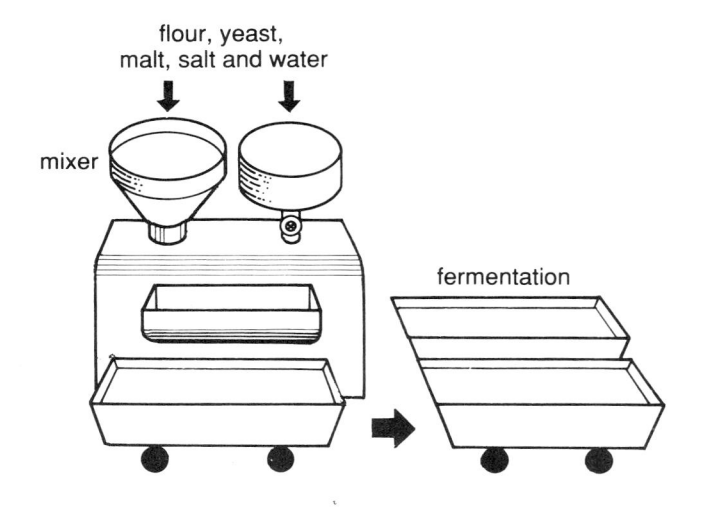

2 The rest of the flour is added and the dough mixed again. A divider cuts the dough into loaf-sized pieces. These are shaped by the rounder.

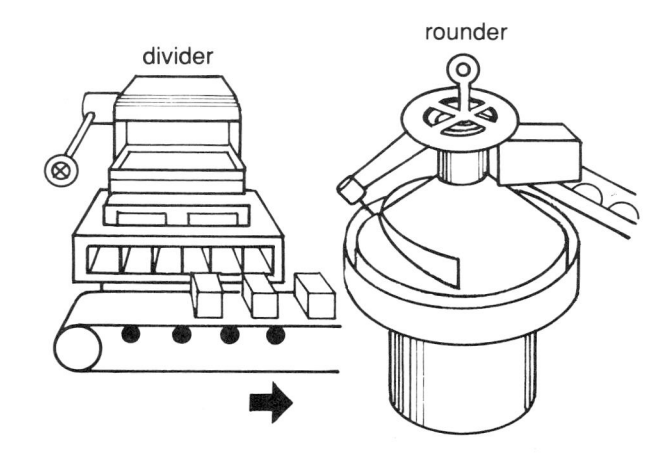

3 A moulder shapes the pieces of dough into cylinders that are put into baking pans. The dough ferments again. It is then put in the oven.

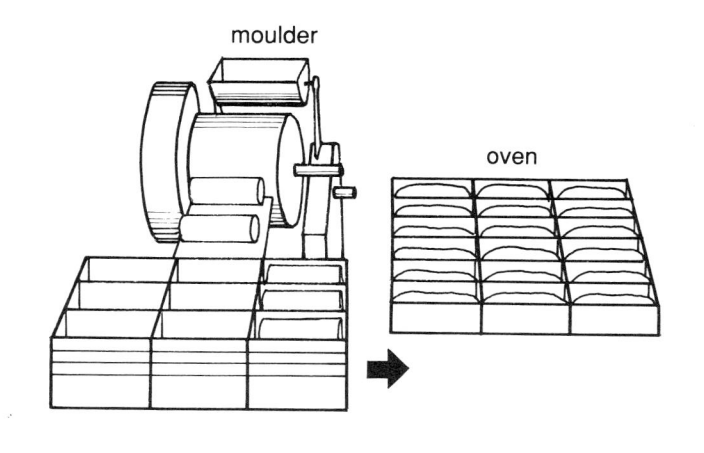

4 The loaves are baked for 20 minutes. They are cooled, sliced and wrapped.

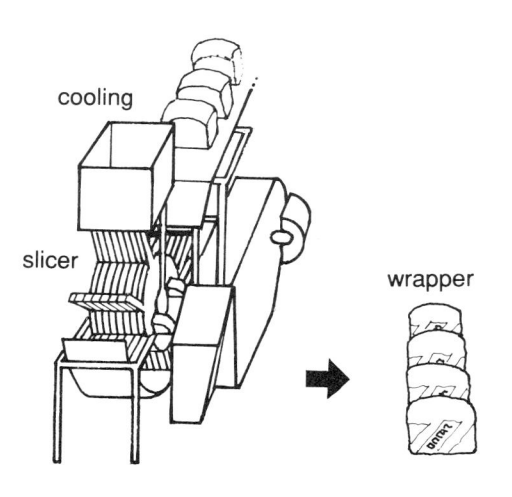

Making biscuits

Enzymes are also used in baking in the production of biscuits. A flour with a relatively low content of protein (gluten) is used, which is not too strong or tough. Sometimes it is difficult to obtain enough of this kind of flour. Often the gluten must be changed by adding a softening agent. Sodium bisulphite is used. Unfortunately, it affects other substances in the flour. For example, the vitamin B1 is completely destroyed.

There is therefore great interest in using a protein-digesting enzyme to soften the gluten. Many different enzymes which work in neutral or slightly acid pHs can be used. There are several suitable protein-digesting enzymes made by fungi and bacteria.

Brewing beer

The cartoon below shows the main stages in brewing beer.

Preparation. Barley is washed... soaked and drained, ...then spread on floors... or loaded in boxes.

Enzyme fermentation. Seeds germinate. Turn and mix occasionally for several days.

Dry in a kiln.....

Crush as required.

Hot water is added to make a mash which is filtered. The liquid is called wort.

Enzymes act on protien and starch

Hops are boiled, cooled and filtered.

The brew is fermented for a few days, clarified, filtered and pasteurised for a keg beer or lager, then put into its final containers...

Or fermented for 3 months to 2 years. Colouring added if required, it is filtered, clarified, pasteurised and bottled...

Then sent to sales outlets.

MORE ABOUT BEER

The production of beer starts with the **malting of barley**. The grain is allowed to sprout in water for a short time. It produces enzymes which catalyze the breakdown of starch to sugar.

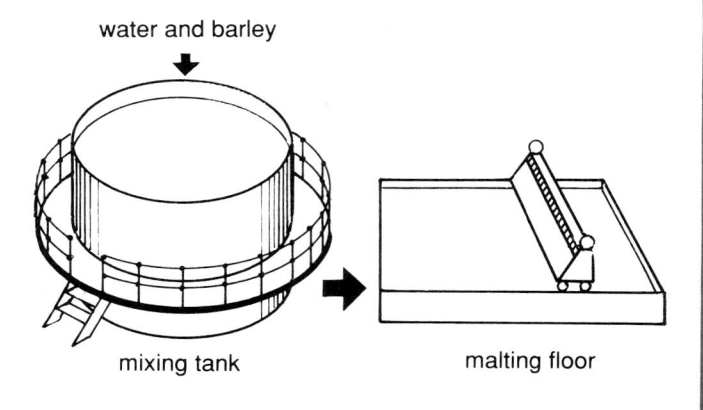

water and barley → mixing tank → malting floor

An extract mixed with water is called **wort**. This is separated and boiled with hops in a **brew kettle**. The boiling extracts flavour from the hops and stops the enzymes working.

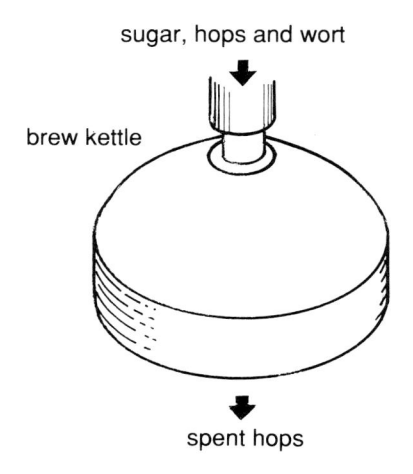

sugar, hops and wort → brew kettle → spent hops

The **malt** (dried germinated barley) is crushed and mixed with warm water. It then goes to the **mash tun**, where the enzymes from the barley continue to break down the starch. The used barley is removed leaving the extract.

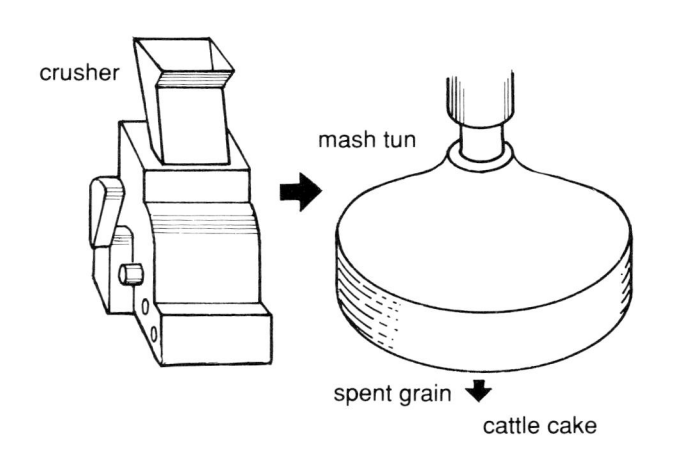

crusher → mash tun → spent grain → cattle cake

The hops are removed and the wort cooled. It is then put into a **fermenter** and yeast is added. After fermentation, the beer may go to a lagering tank to mature. Finally it is pasteurized and bottled.

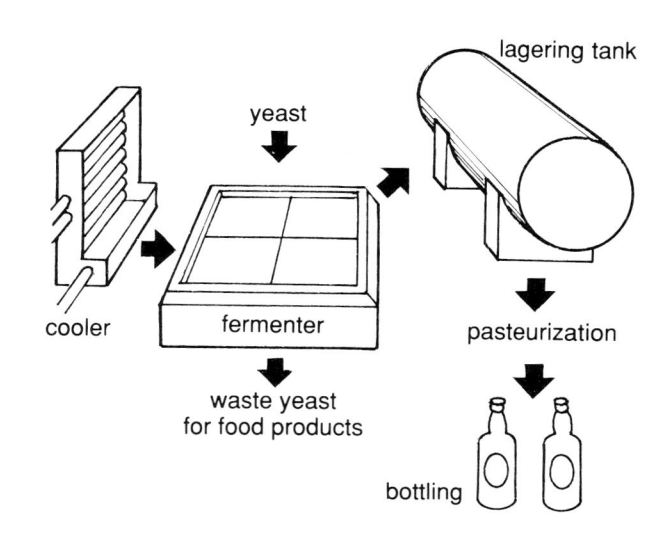

cooler → fermenter (yeast added, waste yeast for food products) → lagering tank → pasteurization → bottling

Batching and continuous fermentation

Beer is brewed in very large volumes. Mash is often in 450 000 litre tanks, so large amounts of starter yeast are needed. To supply all the necessary yeast, the brewer uses a series of cultures of increasing volume. These start with a test tube in the laboratory and end with a starter culture of several hundred litres. This culture is thrown away after use. The cultures must remain pure or a complete batch of beer could be lost. If large volumes of beer are spoiled by contamination from microbes, money will be wasted since the beer cannot be sold. The disposal of the waste beer poses another problem. If the contaminated beer was passed out to a sewage works, it could affect the useful microbes which treat the sewage (see pages 12–13).

Brewing usually takes place in **batches** as just described. However, **continuous fermentation** processes are sometimes used. They consists of two fermentation tanks. Sterilized wort is pumped into the first tank. Yeast grows, producing about half the desired amount of alcohol. In the second tank, the yeast grows less, but more alcohol is produced because the supply of oxygen is restricted. Finally the mixture is cooled. The yeast settles to the bottom. Carbon dioxide is collected from the top and beer from the middle. The carbon dioxide is sold in its solid form as 'dry ice' for refrigeration.

NOW TRY THESE!

1 Name the substances that are represented by the letters A–H below.

industrial brewing

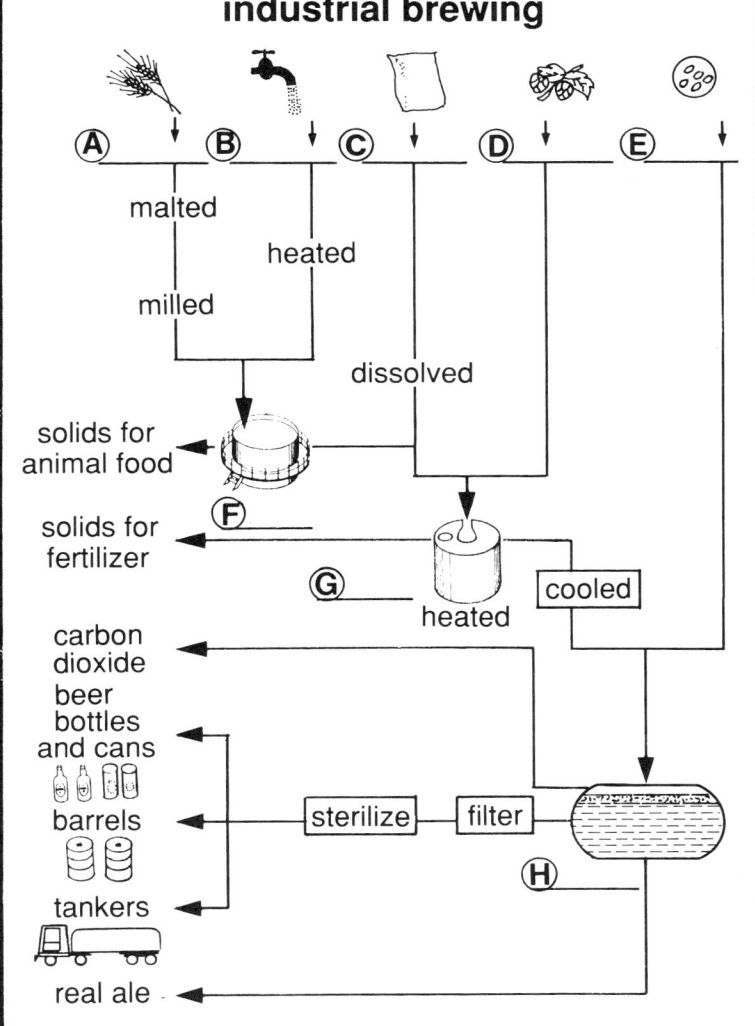

[Flow diagram showing inputs A, B, C, D, E leading through malted, milled, heated, dissolved stages to F (solids for animal food), G (solids for fertilizer), heated, cooled, filter, sterilize, H, producing carbon dioxide, beer bottles and cans, barrels, tankers, real ale]

b
  i Explain why sugar is added to the brew kettle.
  ii Explain the reasons for filtering the beer which comes from the fermenting vessel.
  iii Explain the purpose of the hops.

2 a Below is a flow diagram showing the stages in beer production.

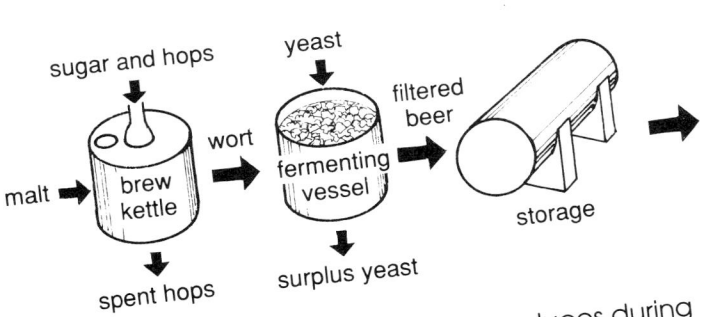

[Diagram: malt → brew kettle (with sugar and hops in, spent hops out) → wort → fermenting vessel (yeast in, surplus yeast out) → filtered beer → storage → bottling]

  i Name two chemicals that yeast produces during fermentation.
  ii Name the group of organisms to which yeast belongs.

c Suggest one use for
  i spent hops **ii** surplus yeast.

d Explain why it is essential to sterilize the storage tank and bottles before using them.

Making Cheese

Little Miss Muffet sat on her tuffet eating her curds and whey...

This popular nursery rhyme is recited by hundreds of children every day. But what are **curds** and **whey**? When milk curdles it separates into a lumpy solid part and a thin watery part. The solid is curd and the liquid is whey. In cheese manufacture, pasteurized milk can be made to curdle in two ways:

a By the addition of **rennet**. This is made from an enzyme, **rennin**, found in calves' stomachs. (Modern methods use an enzyme called **rennilase** which is made by microbes.)

b Sometimes special cultures of microbes are added.

When soft cheeses are made, the whey is just allowed to drain from the curd. For hard chesses, the whey is squeezed out in a cheese press. **Salt** is added to the curd to kill microbes and to give flavour to the cheese. Cottage cheese is just salted curd. All other types of cheese are ripened and flavoured. This is done by adding a variety of microbes to the curd or to the outside of the cheese. For example, blue cheese is infected with fungus to give it flavour.

From milk to cheese

Fresh milk is delivered to the creamery. First it is checked for quality. It is then heat treated and pumped into large vats. A starter culture of the bacterium *Streptococcus thermophilus* is added to speed the ripening process. Adding rennet to the heated milk causes it to clot (coagulate). In modern cheese making on an industrial scale, rennilase is used. This is produced by microorganisms. Rennet or rennilase produces the curd within 6 hours at 31 °C. After 45 minutes the curd is cut into cubes and the whey is run off. The curd is allowed to settle to the bottom of the vat.

The 'cheddaring' process now takes place. This consists of cutting the warm curd into blocks and stacking these on top of each other. The pH falls to between 5.2 and 5.3 which kills harmful bacteria. (They cannot survive in acid conditions.) Piling up the blocks flattens out gas pockets and removes gas from the curd.

Stirring the curd

Draining the curd

A cheddaring tower

Adding salt

Enzymes from active bacteria give the flavour and odour during ripening. They act on many chemicals in the cheese to give the various characteristic tastes and smells. Some cheeses have additional bacteria and fungi added to them, for example Gorgonzola, Blue Stilton, Brie and Camembert. Salt is added to the curd to help preserve the finished cheese. All cheese is inspected as part of quality control before being sold.

Quality control

Boning up on cheese

DID YOU KNOW?

Waste chicken bones could soon be helping some Canadian companies to make cheese. A poultry processing firm wanted to dispose of the unwanted bones cheaply. They formed them into a substance which can hold the bacteria and enzymes needed to make some foods.

The substance is called Biobone. It was developed by Bioprotein, a company in Canada. In cheesemaking, rennin is the enzyme needed to start the process that turns milk into cheese. It is expensive and can only be used once. It is poured into a vat of milk. Because natural rennin is in short supply, some cheesemakers use rennilase, an enzyme made by microbes, which can give the cheese an unpleasant flavour.

If Biobone is placed in rennin, the rennin is held in the porous bone. Milk is pumped through the Biobone to start the cheesemaking process, leaving the rennin behind to be used again.

NOW TRY THESE!

1 Suppose you own a cheese processing factory and you wanted to use Biobone. What would you have to find out before using it as described?

2 Suggest why the demand of natural rennin exceeds it supply.

3 Explain why chicken bones are better to use for Biobone manufacture than bones of mammals.

WASTE WATER

Without a second thought, human beings have treated rivers like sewers and lakes like cesspools. These natural systems struggle to cope with pollution. There are microbes in rivers and lakes which break down moderate amounts of organic matter. However, they can quickly be destroyed by detergents, sewage and effluent from factories. We have had a 'Freedom from Hunger Campaign'. We may also soon need a 'Freedom from Thirst Campaign'. If something is not done to keep fresh water pure, we shall face a desperate situation.

Land needs water in order to feed us, and most industry could not function without it. In advanced industrial countries, each person needs about 300 gallons a day. This is just a drop in the ocean of the water needed by the steel-making and chemical industries. Without food you would probably last more than 15 days. Without water you might last only three. Yet we waste and pollute water every day.

Sweet success

DID YOU KNOW?

The waste water from a sweet factory contained a large amount of sugar. Before 1976 the factory owners were paying £6000 a year to the local water authority to have the sugar removed from the water. Biotechnologists suggested that it would be possible to cut the factory's costs by using microbes to remove the sugar. They added yeast to the waste water. The yeast multiplied so rapidly that it could be collected and sold as animal food. The factory owners were then able to make a profit from their waste sugar, instead of paying the water authority.

NOW TRY THESE!

1 Explain why the waste sugar in the effluent could harm the environment.
2 Explain how the yeast removed the sugar.

Microbes and sewage

About 400 litres of sewage are produced per person per day in large cities in the UK. Only about half a litre of this is the solid which could cause a health risk. The problem stems from the variety of bacteria which live on the solid. Many of them are harmless to humans but can still cause pollution. If they enter rivers or lakes they multiply rapidly and use up the oxygen in the water. This is disastrous to all the organisms in the water which need oxygen (are **aerobic**). The sewage acts as a fertilizer and increases the growth rate of plants in the water. The plants then smother other organisms in the water. They die and decay. This increases the number of bacteria in the water, so reducing further the amount of oxygen. Because of this, untreated sewage can no longer legally be dumped in open pits or poured into water sources in Britain. It must be treated at sewage works.

Plan of a sewage works

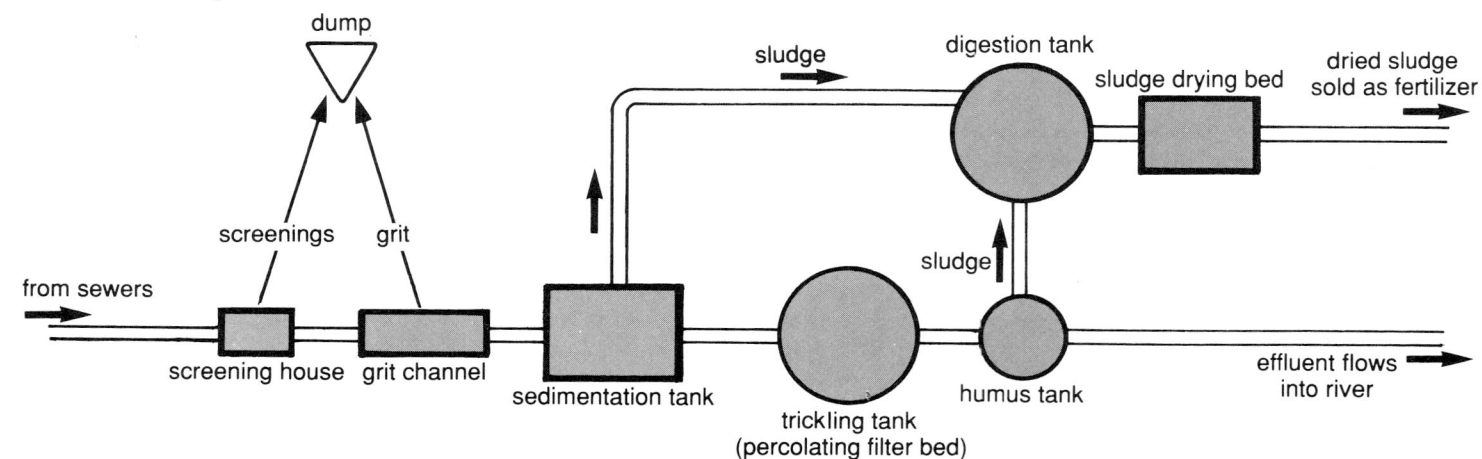

First the sewage is passed through wire **screens**. They collect large objects which would otherwise damage the pumps. Then the sewage flows through **grit channels**. Here grit and gravel and collected. They are relatively heavy and settle to the bottom. They may be washed and used in industry. Most of the remaining solids are organic. They are pumped into large **sedimentation tanks** where they settle to the bottom. A sediment called **sludge** is formed. The processes just described make up **primary treatment**. Some cities do little more than this with their sewage. If they are on the coast they remove the sludge and pump the effluent into the sea. Chlorine is added which kills harmful bacteria. The health risk is thus reduced.

Secondary treatment may be needed in other cities. It is used where the effluent goes into small rivers or streams which would otherwise be affected by the sewage. From the sedimentation tanks the sewage passes into a **trickling tank**. This contains a bed of stones about 180 cm deep. On the stones is a slime of microbes. These are mainly useful bacteria which live on dead matter. The sewage trickles on to the stones from a pipe. The bacteria break down the organic matter to harmless chemicals. Any remaining solids settle out in a **humus tank**. By now, up to 95 per cent of the solids in the sewage have been removed. Chlorine is added to kill any organisms that are still present. The effluent can then be safely pumped into streams. Finally, the solid sludge collected during the treatment is put in large digestion tanks. These are heated to speed up the action of the bacteria in them. The bacteria break down the sludge into harmless material in 30 days. The purified sludge may be dried and sold as fertilizer.

The microbes which are important in sewage treatment are:

- bacteria which break down cellulose
- fungi which break down industrial wastes in acid conditions and destroy nematode worms
- algae which produce oxygen. This helps to kill harmful bacteria which live without oxygen (anaerobic bacteria).

The captivated sludge process

In the 1980s a novel method of waste water treatment became popular. Traditional biological processes use percolating filters or **completely mixed activated sludge** methods. Activated sludge is solid matter from sedimentation tanks mixed with bacteria and Protozoa. The mixture is aerated. It is then passed to percolating filter beds. It then becomes completely mixed activated sludge and thrives, killing harmful anaerobic microbes. The new **captivated sludge** process no longer needs settling tanks to separate the treated effluent from active sludge. Surplus activated sludge can be automatically taken out of the reactor as quickly as is necessary.

In the traditional system the microorganisms are present as films. They can move freely in the waste water. Settling tanks are therefore necessary to separate the films of microorganisms from the treated effluent. The microorganisms are then pumped back to the reactor vessel. In the captivated sludge process, small foam pads are placed in the reactor vessel. These are colonized by microorganisms and never leave the reactor vessel.

Disease and sewage

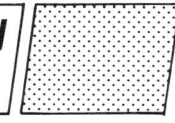

Some diseases can be transmitted in water. Untreated sewage spreads these diseases. They are caused by bacteria, or sometimes by single-celled animals (Protozoa). Bacterial diseases caused in this way include **typhoid, dysentery, cholera** and **food poisoning**. **Amoebic dysentery** is caused by a protozoan which lives in the intestine and passes out of the body in the faeces.

Comparison of the captivated sludge process with the traditional process

feature	captivated sludge process	traditional process
reactor vessel size	minimal	up to five times larger
secondary settlement	not needed	large settling tanks and scraping machinery needed
sludge recycling	not needed	elaborate pumps and pipes needed to return the activated sludge from settlement tanks to reactor vessels
size of works	minimal	more extensive
costs	less hardware – lower price	generally more expensive

Natural Cycles

The nitrogen cycle

Plants need a supply of nitrogen in order to produce proteins and some vitamins. Very few organisms can make use of the abundant nitrogen in the air (see page 3). Plants obtain their nitrogen in nitrates from the soil. However, if all plants kept taking nitrates from the soil, the supply would soon be used up. There is a cycle which ensures that the nitrogen used by plants is put back into the soil. This is called the **nitrogen cycle** and it is summarized below.

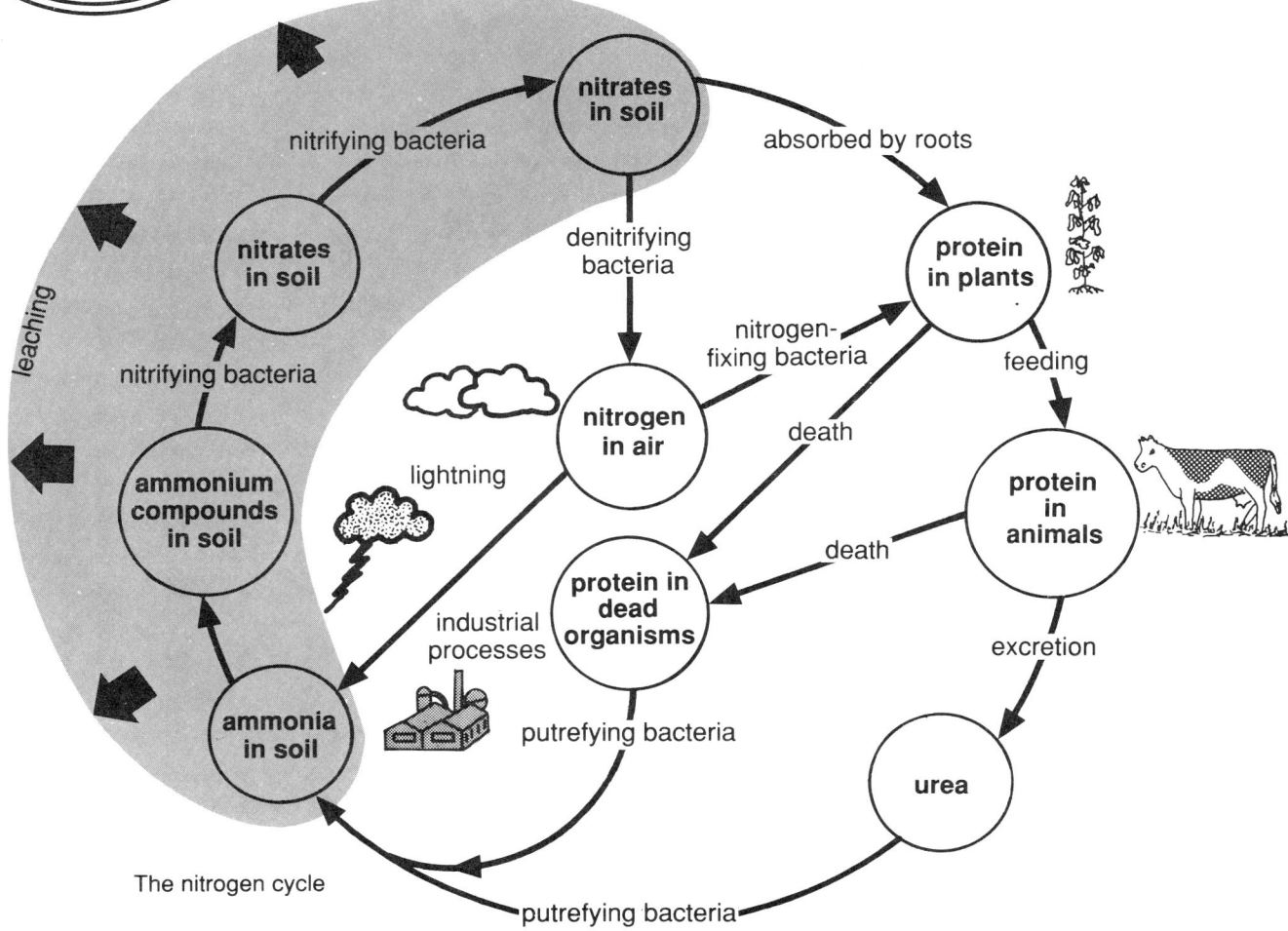

The nitrogen cycle

This complicated looking cycle can be made simpler by separating the building up parts and the breaking down parts. Each uses different types of bacteria. The nitrogen cycle shows how useful bacteria can be to humans. There are many types of bacteria involved, which are essential to all other living organisms as well as us.

Bacteria which build up things in this cycle are:

- **nitrifying bacteria** which build up nitrates from nitrites and ammonium salts
- **nitrogen-fixing bacteria** which are some of the very few organisms which take nitrogen from the air. They change it to a form which can be used by plants to make proteins. They are found in the soil and inside the roots of some special plants. These are the **leguminous** plants which bear pods, e.g. peas, beans, clover, vetch and lupins.

Bacteria which break things down in the cycle are:

- **denitrifying bacteria** which break down nitrates into nitrogen and oxygen. These pass back into the air
- **putrefying bacteria** which are responsible for the decay of dead matter. They break it down to carbon dioxide and ammonia. Ammonia is such a reactive chemical that it forms ammonium salts very quickly in the soil.

The carbon cycle

There is a similar cycle that provides a constant supply of carbon dioxide for plants. The carbon dioxide they use for photosynthesis is returned to the air by animals and bacteria. This cycle is called the **carbon cycle** and is shown on the opposite page.

The carbon cycle

- **carbon dioxide in air**
  - burning – carbon compounds combine with oxygen and produce carbon dioxide
  - photosynthesis – green plants absorb carbon dioxide and water. They produce carbon compounds (sugars, starch etc) and oxygen
  - respiration
- **oxygen in air**
  - respiration – green plants and animals take in oxygen and produce carbon dioxide
- **carbon compounds in green plants**
  - death → **carbon compounds in soil**
  - feeding → **carbon compounds in animals**
- **carbon compounds in fossil fuels (coal, oil, gas, peat)**
  - fossilization
  - decay by bacteria (some use oxygen, all produce carbon dioxide)
  - respiration
- excretion and death

Using the last straw

A cocktail of microbes may soon provide an economic alternative to burning straw. For thousands of years, farmers have used fire to clear land for the next sowing. This kills off crop diseases.

The only real alternatives to burning are either to leave the straw to rot where it is, or to plough it into the soil. Both methods can lead to an increase in disease. They also cause difficulties for seed drilling machines.

Bacterial activity in the soil is normally limited by the lack of a ready source of energy. Straw contains large quantities of cellulose. Microbes can break down cellulose to simple sugars. These can then be used by nitrogen-fixing bacteria. Scientists have selected several microbes for this purpose. For example, there is a fungus which lives on other fungi that cause disease in root crops. This fungus can also break down cellulose. One nitrogen-fixing bacterium does the same. Yet another bacterium produces large amounts of gum which binds soil particles together. The oxygen consumption of this bacterium also helps provide the right conditions for the nitrogen-fixing bacteria.

These microbes are all mixed together to form a cocktail. The cocktail can be sprayed on to straw and the straw is then ploughed into the soil.

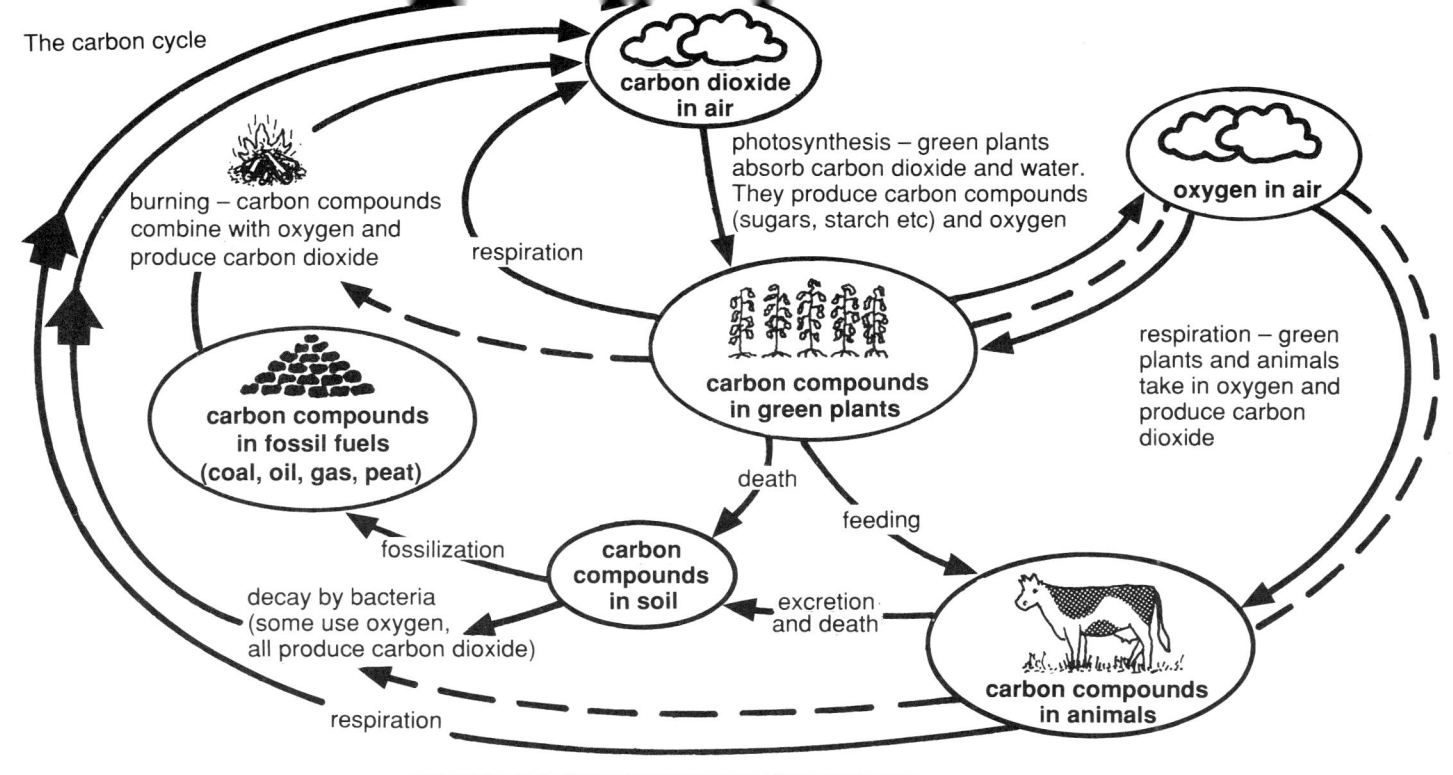

DID YOU KNOW?

Bacteria clean up

Researchers in West Germany are perfecting a technique to rid drinking water of nitrates. They are using bacteria. Agriculture has led to rising levels of nitrates in ground water. Scientists believe that there may be a link between nitrates in drinking water and stomach cancer. High levels of nitrates can also cause anaemia in newborn infants. Scientists have successfully shown that a species of bacteria can eliminate nitrates from water. The water industry could find this process economical. The bacteria convert the nitrates to harmless nitrogen so there is no poisonous waste water left.

NOW TRY THESE!

1 Explain why agriculture has been responsible for an increase in nitrates in ground water.
2 Which of the following types of bacteria is responsible for the action described above?
- putrefying
- denitrifying
- nitrifying
- nitrogen-fixing

NOW TRY THESE!

1 Explain how the spray acts as
  i a decomposer ii a fertilizer
  iii a fungicide.
2 Suggest how the spray would protect the soil against erosion.
3 What is meant by 'the right conditions' for the nitrogen-fixing bacteria?

Most of the energy we use in industry and at home is released from oil, coal natural gas and wood. There is an increasing amount of nuclear energy being used, but this involves the risk of radiation leaks. These sources of energy are either becoming scarce or can damage our environment.

There's an awful lot of sugar in Brazil!

Microbes can produce fuels from waste material. These fuels can be used without danger to the environment. In Brazil, sugar cane is converted into alcohol by microbes. Yeast is used to ferment the sugar which produces the alcohol.

The alcohol is then separated from the yeast by filtering. The filter allows the alcohol and water to pass through but keeps the yeast back. The alcohol can then be separated from water by **distillation**. Alcohol boils at a lower temperature than water. When the mixture is heated, the alcohol evaporates out first. When the vapour is cooled it forms liquid alcohol again and can be collected in a different container. Pure alcohol will burn in the same way as petrol. It can be used in specially adapted car engines and does not pollute the atmosphere.

An alcohol-powered car

NOW TRY THESE!

1 Fill in the blanks:

When alcohol is first made from sugar it is mixed with _____ cells and water. To separate the yeast we must _____ the mixture. The _____ cannot pass through. Only the water and _____ pass into a collecting vessel. Alcohol has a _____ boiling point than water.

2 a State four sources of energy used today.

 b Give two reasons why we should try to find other sources of energy.

 c What microbes would you use to produce alcohol?

 d What unusual use does Brazil make of alcohol?

 e Why is it a good idea for Brazil to use sugar cane to make alcohol?

 f Would it be a good idea to turn sugar into alcohol in Scotland? Why?

Plant power

DID YOU KNOW?

Research is taking place to produce algae which can be converted to petrol. Scientists in Colorado are studying thousands of types of algae called diatoms to see if they can produce large amounts of fats and oils. These can be converted into fuels. The algae are grown in tanks with added carbon dioxide, nitrates and phosphates.

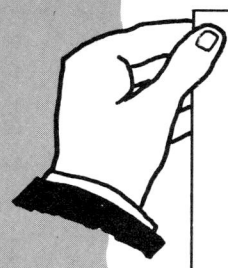

Now try these!

a What is the purpose of adding **i** carbon dioxide and **ii** nitrates and phosphates to the tanks containing the algae?

b What other factors are needed for the healthy growth of the algae?

ENGINE OIL

DID YOU KNOW?

In 1980 biotechnologists in Brazil began to experiment with palm oil as a source of fuel for vehicles. Buses used a fuel which was a mixture of diesel oil (73%), palm oil (20%) and ethanol (7%). Palms can be harvested throughout the year. It is easier to extract oil from the oil palm than to make ethanol from sugar. Water is not needed and the waste product is rich in protein.

Now try these!

1. Give four advantages of obtaining fuel from palm oil rather than from sugar cane.
2. Suggest how the waste product of the process could be used.
3. Why would it be uneconomic to produce fuel in this way in Scotland?

Energy from Microbes

Biogas, produced by microbes, and **natural gas** from the North Sea, are both **methane**. Rotting plants in ponds and marshes produce biogas. In China and India, plant waste and animal dung are fermented to produce biogas. It is used for cooking and lighting (on a relatively small scale). In Britain, refuse dumps produce large amounts of methane, but most of it is wasted. However, in Dundee, enough methane escapes from the dumps to fuel the large Ninewells Hospital.

Why some microbes make methane

One of the reasons living things need food is as a source of energy. Green plants can make their own food. They use energy from the sun and the green substance **chlorophyll**. This process is called **photosynthesis**:

| light + carbon dioxide + water — chlorophyll → food + oxygen |
| (from the air)   (from the soil) |

Energy is released from food by respiration:

| food + oxygen ⟶ energy + carbon dioxide + water |

As you can see, respiration is almost the exact reverse of photosynthesis.

Some microbes can release energy from food without oxygen. Certain microbes which do this produce methane as a waste product. They live where there is very little (or no) air, for example, in deep underwater mud and in the bodies of dead plants and animals.

| food (decaying organisms) ⟶ energy + methane |

Where there are marshes, some methane is released into the air as marsh gas. This burns easily. It makes a good fuel. The methane gas is a waste product from the microbes, but it is useful to us and we can produce energy from it.

Marsh gas

Production of biogas

NOW TRY THESE!

1. Name the processes by which living things get energy from their food.
2. Which gas is needed to release this energy?
3. Name two places where methane-making microbes might live.
4. What is unusual about these places?
5. How would you show that methane contains energy?
6. Explain why we say that methane is a 'waste product' from the microbes.
7. Why is it useful to be able to produce methane in countries like China and India?

DID YOU KNOW?

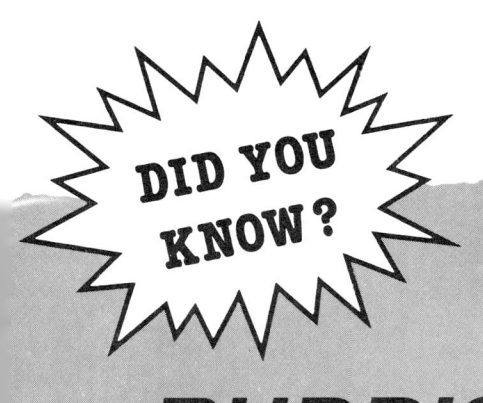

RUBBISH!

The Meriden rubbish tip near Coventry takes 3500 tonnes of domestic and industrial waste every day. It produces 2 cubic metres of gas per minute. The gas is collected in pipes. Any hydrogen sulphide is removed from it. It is compressed with air and fed to a turbine. The turbine drives electric generators, giving 3.5 megawatts of power. Throughout Britain, 669 tips are large enough to collect gas from and these could fuel 5 per cent of the electricity used in Britain.

A land-fill rubbish tip

NOW TRY THESE!

1 What gas do you think is collected and used as fuel?
2 List the energy changes described in the account.

DID YOU KNOW?

RUSSIANS DO IT SAFELY!

In Russia, bacteria from rivers, lakes and the sea bed have been grown in salt water in 'microbe factories'. The solution is then pumped through boreholes in coal seams and sprayed on the coal face. Six months later the miners start mining there. Microbes break down methane at the coal face, reducing the level by 50 per cent. This means less danger for the miners. It also means the mines do not have to be ventilated, so saves time too.

NOW TRY THESE!

1 Why is methane normally dangerous for miners?
2 Why do you think the solution of microbes is pumped into the mine six months before mining begins?

Food from Microbes

Microbe pie

Most people think of food as tins and packets on a supermarket shelf. Most of our food comes from large animals like sheep and chickens or large plants like wheat and beans. Microbes have been used as **part** of food (e.g. in yogurt and cheese) for thousands of years. Scientists are now trying to make food completely from microbes.

Yogurt and cheese are made using microbes

One-fifth of the food you eat should be protein. This is essential because it is used for growth and repair. In poor countries, many people do not get enough protein. They may suffer from the disease **kwashiorkor** because of this. If you eat enough meat or certain fruits and vegetables, you get enough protein. In some countries, protein is expensive because the soil is too poor to grow the crops which contain protein.

Scientists are now working on ways of making protein from bacteria and fungi. Some countries like Britain and Russia are producing large amounts of protein using **fermenters**. 'Meat' pies could soon be made partly from microbe protein as well as beef or chicken.

The microbes are fed all they need in a large container (a fermenter). The microbes need:

food + minerals + oxygen + water

They reproduce many times. They are then drained off and filtered out of the liquid. The resulting protein is then processed into food for animals or humans.

△ Large animals produce our meat
▽ Kwashiorkor

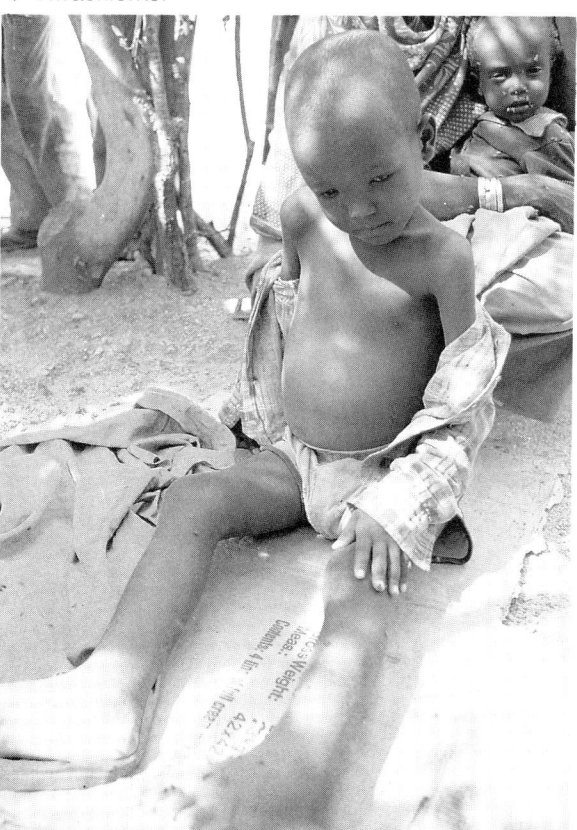

From fungus to spaghetti bolognese

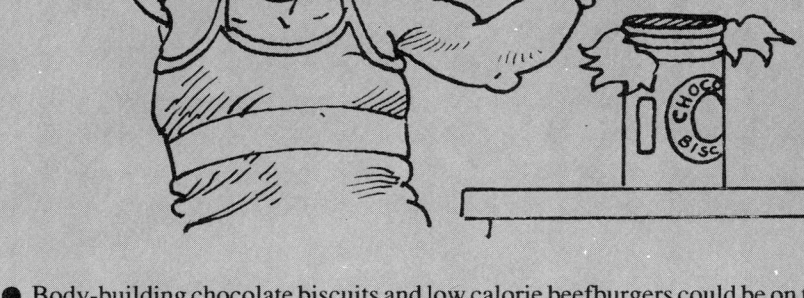

DID YOU KNOW?

The Pruteen factory at ICI Billingham on Teeside

- Body-building chocolate biscuits and low calorie beefburgers could be on the way thanks to research by a food company. Rank Hovis McDougall (RHM), makers of Britain's most popular brands of food, and Imperial Chemical Industries (ICI) have joined forces to sell food products made from a fungus!

- RHM have spent ten years making myco-protein, on a small scale, but further development is taking place in ICI's pilot factory. This was built to make ICI's animal food, Pruteen. This factory can make 1000 tonnes a year. However, RHM hopes to move into ICI's larger factory. This can make 20 000 tonnes of myco-protein a year which will make the process more economical.

- Myco-protein comes from a fungus belonging to the same group as mushrooms. RHM ferments the fungus and harvests it. Further treatment turns it into a food which can be used. The myco-protein fungus doubles its weight every 5 hours when fed with glucose syrup at 30 °C in the fermenter.

- Myco-protein is even better than steak in some ways! Look at the table below to see how. (Some types of fats clog up blood vessels. Fibre helps the digestive system work properly.)

	Percentage of weight without water	
	myco-protein	lean steak
protein	44.3	68.2
fat	13.8	30.2
fibre	37.6	0

Now try these!

1. Which class of food is needed for body building?
2. How much of your diet should be made up of body-building foods?
3. Why is it unusual to have much body-building food in chocolate biscuits?
4. Why would low calorie beefburgers be better for you than high calorie beefburgers?
5. 100 g of the fungus that makes myco-protein was left at 30 °C in glucose syrup. How much fungus would you expect there to be after 5 hours?
6. What conditions does the fungus that makes myco-protein need to be healthy?
7. Explain why myco-protein can be better for you than steak.

NEW FOODS

More about myco-protein – a new food

Myco-protein is a protein- and fibre-rich food from a fungus. The 'myco' part of the name comes from 'mycology' which is the study of fungi. This word is derived from the Greek *mukes* which means mushroom. Myco-protein is made by a type of fungus called *Fusarium graminearum*. Work has been in progress since 1964 to perfect the large-scale production of myco-protein. It is made from carbohydrate using a continuous fermentation process (see page 9).

Wheat starch is a carbohydrate. It is in plentiful supply because it is a waste product from the production of wheat protein (gluten). Gluten is separated from wheat flour and used in vast amounts to make different foods.

The fungus is grown in a fermenter in a liquid substrate under aerobic conditions. The substrate contains starch and other substances which help it grow, including a variety of minerals.

Protein which is made by microbes and intended for human food must have low levels of ribonucleic acid (RNA). Heating to 65 °C removes RNA. The harvested myco-protein is a buff coloured slurry which smells of mushrooms. After pasteurization, it is processed into food products, especially pies.

Fibre foods?

Quorn – a new food

Quorn is the brand name of a versatile new food that is high in protein and fibre, low in fats and cholesterol free. Developed over 20 years it can now be made on a commercial scale. It has undergone extensive consumer testing. Quorn's excellent nutritional balance and delicious taste make it exactly the right food for today's increasingly diet conscious environment. With a cost equivalent to that of prime cuts of cooked meats, Quorn is not a cheap meat substitute. It can be used in a variety of savoury products as an alternative to meat and poultry. It can also be used to create totally new foods.

DID YOU KNOW?

The Soviet Union is turning to biotechnology to tackle its food shortages. Russian scientists are looking at any likely source of new foodstuffs, including cotton! Turning cotton into simpler food sugars often needs harsh chemicals. These break down the tough fibres and digest the cellulose. It is then expensive to remove the chemicals. A better method is to use a more gentle chemical treatment followed by a bath of enzymes, nature's catalysts. These 'chew up' the cellulose. The process uses enzymes produced by bacteria. It takes at least two months to produce 90 000 tonnes of glucose.

Now try these!

1 What is meant by 'consumer testing'? Explain why it is essential before marketing a new food product.

2 What is meant by 'a diet conscious environment'? Suggest why myco-protein would satisfy the demands of such an environment.

3 Explain how cotton could be a valuable source of myco-protein in the Soviet Union.

Food from waste

Surplus yeast is available as a waste product from brewing industries. It is a very valuable source of food. Yeast extract makes up the familiar Marmite – a paste you spread on bread or use to enrich other foods with vitamins. More recently another food source, microorganisms, have been grown on various wastes from agriculture and industry. The different substances used are listed below.

substance	source	organisms
cellulose	plant wastes	yeasts, fungi
starch grains	plant wastes	yeasts, fungi
potato wastes	potato products	yeasts, fungi
sulphites	paper industry	yeasts, fungi
whey	dairy industry	yeasts
molasses	sugar industry	yeasts
methane	natural gas	bacteria
methanol	natural gas	bacteria
ethanol	oil	yeasts
paraffins	oil	yeasts
minerals	natural source	algae

These processes have the advantage of using raw materials which would otherwise be thrown away. They have the added bonus that the waste water produced is cleaner and produces less pollution than disposing of the raw materials would. A more recent development has been the growth of microbes on a variety of products made from fossil fuels. Methane, methanol, ethanol and paraffins have all been investigated as possible substances on which to grow microorganisms.

The basic ideas is to change relatively cheap natural resources into valuable goods rather than to simply burn them as fuels. Alternative sources of food are needed because of the population explosion, the energy crisis and uncertainties about world harvests of cereals. At present, agriculture produces sufficient food to avoid widespread starvation. However, poor countries cannot pay for the food so starvation is still a problem in many places. Biotechnology cannot solve this problem directly but it can help where waste products or fossil fuels are available. At present bacteria, yeasts, other fungi and micro-algae are being investigated as alternatives or supplements to the normal diet of humans and domestic animals. As these microorganisms are rich in protein they are often called single cell protein (SCP). Scientists hope they will form a protein rich supplement to replace the traditional protein rich products like soya beans and fish meal (which may soon become scarce due to over-fishing). The more wealthy nations have a high demand for animal protein. This, however, is wasteful of energy. The domestic animals use up energy when they convert plant proteins into their own proteins. It would conserve energy if plant proteins or single cell protein were eaten by humans.

All new foods must be tested for possible toxic side effects, as new drugs would be. There could also be problems involved in marketing SCP as human food. The flavour, the colour and the texture must be just right or people will not want to eat it. Also, some people might not like the idea of eating microorganisms. Animals are less fussy, though the food must still be tested for side effects.

WASTE DISPOSAL AND MINING

Biotechnology provides us with a way of disposing of waste products safely. So it can help us with the pollution problems that we create. Microbes have been used for many years to make sewage harmless (see pages 12–13). They can even help clear up the mess we make when oil is spilled at sea. Fertilizer can be made by giving starter cultures of bacteria to garden compost heaps.

In each of these examples microbes are recycling materials for us. Because many of our resources are in limited supply, this recycling is very important. However, we can also use bacteria to break down metal-containing rocks called **ores**. The metal is dissolved in a liquid and then drained away. We call the process **bioleaching**. The metal can be extracted from the liquid and purified.

Certain microbes can concentrate metals inside themselves. Some algae and bacteria accumulate metals from the water surrounding them. Dissolved salts of every known element are found in the sea. In fact, most of the world's gold and silver are in the sea. Some rare elements like vanadium are concentrated in the bodies of animals called sea squirts. In the future, it may be feasible for biotechnologists to collect rare and precious elements from marine organisms. Already, biotechnologists are finding ways to recover and recycle valuable metals from places where once it was thought impossible.

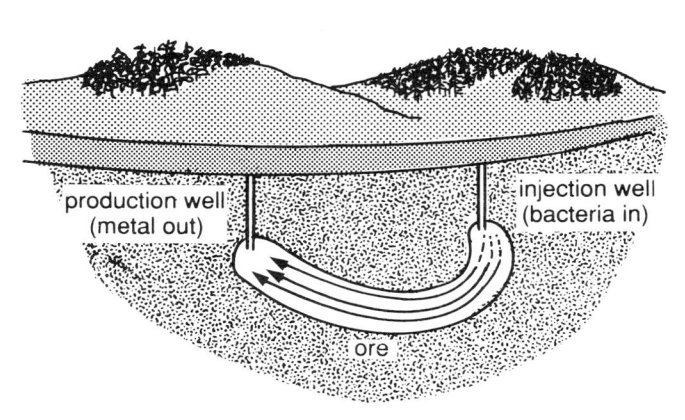

Using bacteria in a mine

Mining with bacteria

Recovery of valuable metals

Deposits of many high grade ores (those containing large amounts of metals) are decreasing at an alarming rate. Methods of mining low grade ores are often very expensive. Microbial mining may be the answer to this problem. Biotechnologists have been studying the biology of the bacterium *Thiobacillus ferro-oxidans*. It finds all its nutrients in carbon dioxide from the air and in mineral salts. It is now used on a large scale in copper mining because it oxidizes insoluble copper ore. It converts it into soluble copper sulphate. Sulphuric acid is a by-product, and it helps to keep the acid conditions (low pH) which the bacteria like. The bacteria can be used on copper waste tips containing as little as 0.25 per cent copper.

Low grade uranium ore (0.02 per cent uranium) has been mined in some parts of the world by a similar method. Mining costs have been cut by 75 per cent in Canada. The rock face is hosed down to encourage microbial growth and the resulting solution is pumped out. The bacterium *Pseudomonas* is being studied with a view to extracting cobalt, nickel and vanadium.

Using enzymes to recover silver

Any exposed photographic film, for example X-ray film, has a layer of gelatine (a protein) containing silver grains stuck to one side of a transparent celluloid base. Silver is expensive, so the photographic industry does not want to throw it away. The silver can be recovered using an enzyme, **trypsin**. Alternatively, biotechnologists use other protein-digesting enzymes specially produced by genetically engineered bacteria (see page 26).

DID YOU KNOW?

End toxic waste

Microbiologists think that there are dozens of species of bacteria capable of breaking down poisonous chemicals. Already they have found microbes to break down all the main classes of dangerous chemicals found in tips. Some of these bacteria need oxygen. In 1974 a scientist patented a process to provide oxygen and salts of nitrogen and phosphorus to microbes in the soil. This encourages them to break down oil-based pollutants, such as many solvents and pesticides.

NOW TRY THESE!

What are the functions of
1 oxygen
2 phosphorus and nitrogen?

NOW TRY THESE!

Tubes A–D were set up as in the diagram opposite with the following contents:

tube A	tube B	tube C	tube D
2 cm^3 distilled water	2 cm^3 acid	2 cm^3 alkali	2 cm^3 distilled water
2 cm^3 enzyme	2 cm^3 enzyme	2 cm^3 enzyme	2 cm^3 boiled enzyme

The tubes were kept at 37 °C for 15 minutes. Each photographic strip was then rubbed 20 times under a running tap. The results were as follows:

tube	appearance of solution	appearance of film after rubbing
A	fairly cloudy	film just becoming transparent
B	clear, colourless	film remained the same
C	very cloudy grey	film completely transparent
D	clear, colourless	film remained the same

1 In which tubes did protein digestion take place?
2 What effect does boiling have on the protein-digesting enzyme?
3 Under what conditions did the protein-digesting enzyme work best?
4 Why were the tubes kept at 37 °C?
5 Suggest how biotechnology could be applied to recovering silver from photographic film.

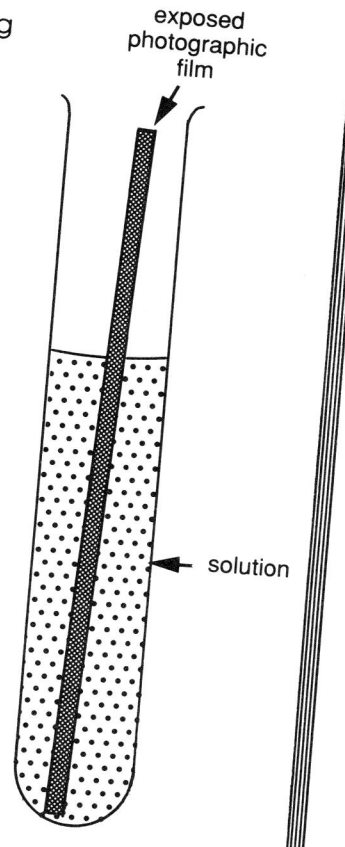

Reprogramming Microbes

How genetic engineering saves lives

Genetic engineering in a nutshell

Genetic engineering means isolating a gene from one organism and putting it in another. In biotechnology scientists often isolate the human genes that make human cells produce, for example, **hormones** (e.g. insulin) or blood proteins. They insert these genes into bacteria or yeasts.

The idea of transferring the human gene to the bacteria is to increase production. The microbes grow relatively cheaply in large fermenters, providing almost unlimited amounts of substances that are practically unobtainable in bulk in any other way.

Genetic engineering starts with the biologist using biological 'scissors' called **restriction enzymes**. These cut chains of **deoxyribose nucleic acid (DNA)** at specific points. The DNA chains are present in **chromosomes**, thread-like structures in the cell's nucleus. With the restriction enzymes the biologist carves out very precisely the gene that he or she wants from the hundreds of others in the nucleus of the cell. The next stage is to insert the gene into a bacterium. It is not put directly into the bacterial chromosome. Instead, genetic engineers use a circular piece of DNA called a **plasmid**. These are normally present in bacteria but are largely independent of the rest of the cell. Plasmids, like chromosomes, carry bacterial genes which control the microbe's metabolism.

The plasmid is cut open with restriction enzymes and the foreign gene inserted. The break is sealed with another enzyme called a **ligase** (an enzyme which binds chemicals together). This process creates a **hybrid** (mixed) molecule called **recombinant DNA**.

The altered (**infective**) plasmids are then mixed in a test tube with bacteria which do not have any plasmids. Some plasmids move inside these bacteria. The infective plasmids carry the foreign gene inside the cell where it can instruct it to make the required protein. The cells are then called **mutants**. The process is shown in the diagram opposite. The experiment is usually regarded as a success only when the gene is **expressed**. This means that the host cell obeys the instructions carried by the foreign gene and manufactures human proteins.

Insulin production

Insulin is a chemical called a **hormone** or 'chemical messenger'. Its function is to keep the concentration of glucose in the blood at a constant level (0.1 g per 100 cm^3 of blood). If the glucose level falls much below this, the body does not have enough glucose to release energy. A glucose level above 0.1 g per 100 cm^3 also disturbs body functions. In particular, the ability of the kidneys to reabsorb glucose is lost and glucose appears in the urine. The body is eventually drained of fuel.

A gland in the abdomen, called the **pancreas**, normally makes insulin. It helps to keep the concentration of glucose

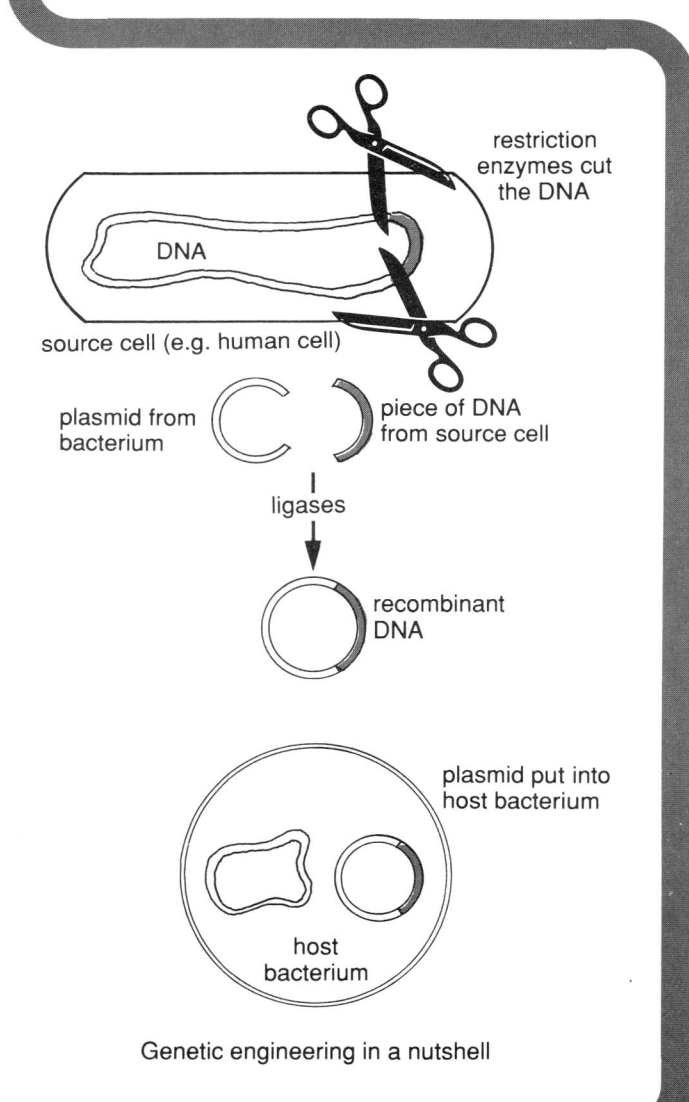

Genetic engineering in a nutshell

constant by changing excess glucose into an insoluble carbohydrate called **glycogen**. This is stored in the liver. Without enough insulin people cannot control their glucose level and suffer from **diabetes**. Fortunately, it is possible to control this condition by injecting pure insulin into a diabetic person.

Until recently the insulin used for this treatment was taken from the pancreas of pigs and cattle. It was difficult to produce enough insulin this way. Genetic engineers have solved the problem of mass production of insulin using bacteria. The method is summarized in the flow diagram opposite.

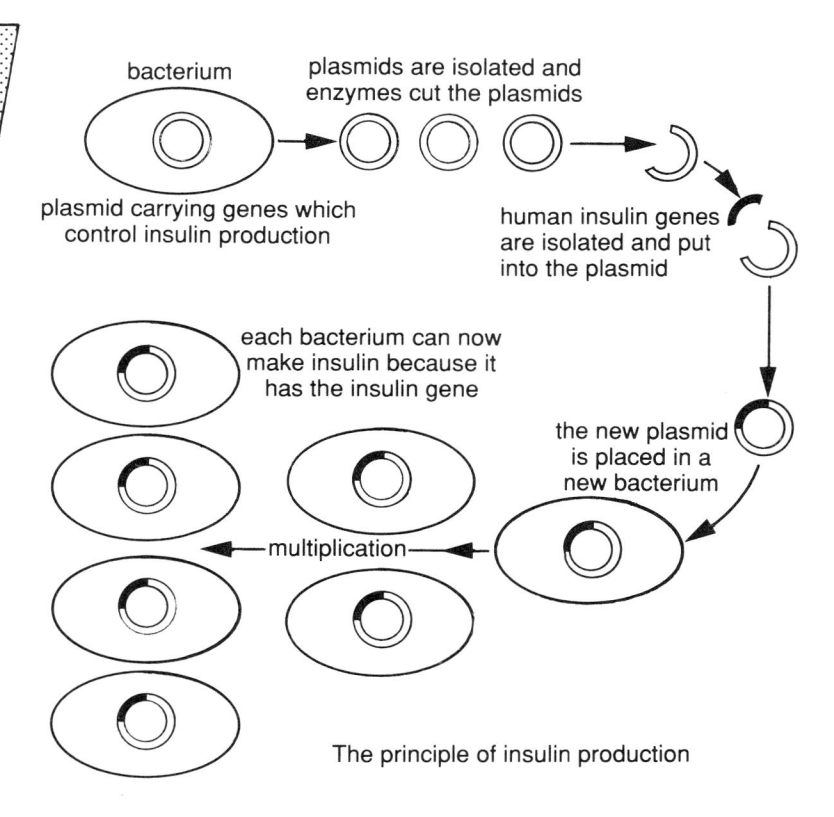

The principle of insulin production

Do-it-yourself pesticides

Biologists have grown a tobacco plant that makes its own pesticide. A Belgian genetic engineering company has modified the genes of a tobacco plant so that it produces a toxin that kills insects.

The gene which controls the manufacture of the toxin has been isolated from a bacterium. It has been inserted into the tobacco plant in two ways:

- The cellulose cell walls of some of the leaf cells were broken down so that the plasmid could pass freely into the cytoplasm.
- Fragments of the stem were wounded with preparations containing the genetically altered plasmids.

NOW TRY THESE!

1 Suggest how the cellulose cell walls of the tobacco cells might have been broken down.
2 Do you think there are possible dangers to the environment involved in this technique?

Mutants in Australia

DID YOU KNOW?

The releasing of genetically engineered microorganisms into the environment to control plant production is about to spead to Australia. A scientist at the Waite Agricultural Research Institute in Adelaide received final clearance from the university to do his research. He wants to soak the roots of almond seedlings in a solution of genetically altered bacteria to treat crown gall disease in roots. After completing the four month experiment, he will sterilize and dispose of the affected soil.

NOW TRY THESE!

1 Explain why the scientist sterilized the soil before disposing of it.
2 Suggest how the sterilization could be carried out.
3 Discuss why environmentalists might oppose the introduction of mutant bacteria into the environment.
4 Suggest how the bacteria would be able to combat crown gall disease (a disease caused by a bacterium) in plant roots.

Enzymes ~ builders and breakers

When chemical reactions take place in cells, enzymes control which substances are used, which products are made and the speed of the reactions.

Enzymes are all proteins. They can
a release energy from our fuel
b bring about growth
c control how we think
d digest food.

Products containing or made of enzymes

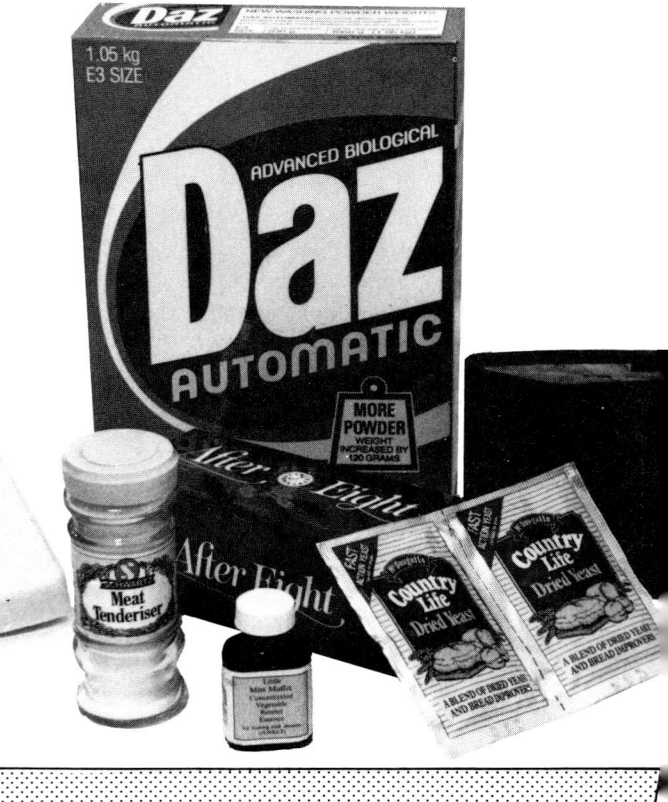

Making use of enzymes

Biotechnologists can take enzymes out of cells and use them to make things and to break things. Here is a selection of products. Some have been made with the help of enzymes; others contain enzymes which make them work.

NOW TRY THESE!

1 What type of chemicals are enzymes?
2 Why are enzymes sometimes called 'chemical controllers'?
3 List three jobs that enzymes do in living things.
4 Look at the photograph of manufactured products. Think how each one is connected with enzymes, then complete a table like the one below.

enzymes are used to make these	these contain working enzymes

More about enzymes

Enzymes are the most important substances in biotechnology. Scientists can grow bacteria and fungi so that they produce enzymes which people can use to do jobs efficiently for them. Biotechnologists have to know how enzymes work, where to find them, and the conditions in which they work best.

NOW TRY THESE!

1 Here is a list of words to do with enzymes. Use the figure or word in the box you think fits best to fill in the spaces below:

| product(s) | alkaline | proteins | cold | 90 °C | optimum | substrate | –ase |
| faster | catalysts | 7 | speed | hot | 37 °C | acid | specific | water |

a Enzymes are _____, i.e. they _____ up a reaction without themselves being used up.

b Enzymes belong to the group of chemicals called _____.

c Enzymes will only work when they are surrounded by _____.

d Most enzymes work best in warm conditions; yours work at body temperature, i.e._____.

e Enzymes do not normally work well in very _____ or _____ conditions.

f Enzymes are permanently damaged by temperatures above _____.

g The temperature at which an enzyme works most efficiently is called its _____ temperature.

h Enzymes do not work very well in _____ or _____ conditions.

i The pH at which enzymes work best is called their _____ pH.

j The more enzyme there is present when a reaction is going on, the _____ the reaction will take place.

k Enzymes are _____, i.e. one enzyme will only catalyze one type of reaction.

l The specific substance an enzyme reacts with is called a _____, and what the enzyme helps to make is called a _____.

m The names of specific enzymes end in _____.

2 How enzymes are affected by pH

A large number of enzymes are now used in industry. Each enzyme carries out a particular chemical reaction quickly, efficiently and without leaving harmful wastes. However, conditions need to be right for them to work. You have already found that an enzyme solution works less well if it is boiled. Boiling has upset the working of the enzyme.

The pH at which an enzyme operates best is called its **optimum pH**. If conditions are too acid or too alkaline, it does not work so well.

For example, the American food industry uses an important enzyme called AG for short which makes glucose syrup from maize (sweetcorn). If an experiment was done to find out how much glucose the enzyme AG could produce at several different pHs, the results would look like those in the table.

Plot a graph of mass of glucose produced against pH of the reaction. What is the optimum pH for the enzyme being used?

pH	glucose produced (milligrams per minute)
4	0.1
5	0.3
6	0.8
7	1.5
8	2.1
9	1.2
10	0.2
12	0.0

Enzymes in Industry

Enzymes can be used cheaply in industry because they do not require high temperatures in order to work. Therefore fuel costs for industrial processes are reduced considerably.

We have already seen industries that use enzymes, e.g. the brewing and dairy industries. However, the best known application of enzymes to most people is probably detergents. We see biological detergents advertised constantly and since the mid 1960s the detergent industry has been the largest of all enzyme users. In the 1970s consumers became painfully aware of allergies to some washing powders containing enzymes. The most widely used enzymes in detergents are all made by bacteria. They are:

- **alcalase** – works best at pH 7–10. Digests protein.
- **esperase** – works best at pH 10–12. Digests protein.
- **savinase** – works best at pH 10–12. Digests protein.
- **termamyl** – works in a pH of up to 9.5 and at a temperature of up to 90 °C. Digests carbohydrates.

Now try these!

Bio-clenz is a washing powder which contains enzymes. The enzymes digest certain stains.

1 Explain why enzymes are often called **biological catalysts**.
2 At 20 °C clothes soaked in *Bio-clenz* need 12 hours to remove stains. Explain why the same clothes only need 3 hours in the same concentration of *Bio-clenz* to remove stains at 40 °C.
3 Explain why *Bio-clenz* does not remove stains at 80 °C.
4 On a box of *Bio-clenz* there is the instruction:

   Important: rinse your hands after contact with this product

   Why is this warning necessary?

Immobilized enzymes

Most enzymes used by industry have been taken from cells and are soluble. These do their work in **batch** systems, i.e. once the reaction is over the products are extracted and the enzymes are thrown away. Such processes are wasteful. The enzymes can be **immobilized** in insoluble substances which still allow the substrate to react with the enzyme. The enzyme can then be recovered at the end of the process. In industry these insoluble substances are fixed to permanent supports. The substrate is trickled over them. The products trickle out at the other end. The enzyme stays in the system. This is a **continuous system** because there is no need to stop it to separate the enzyme and the products.

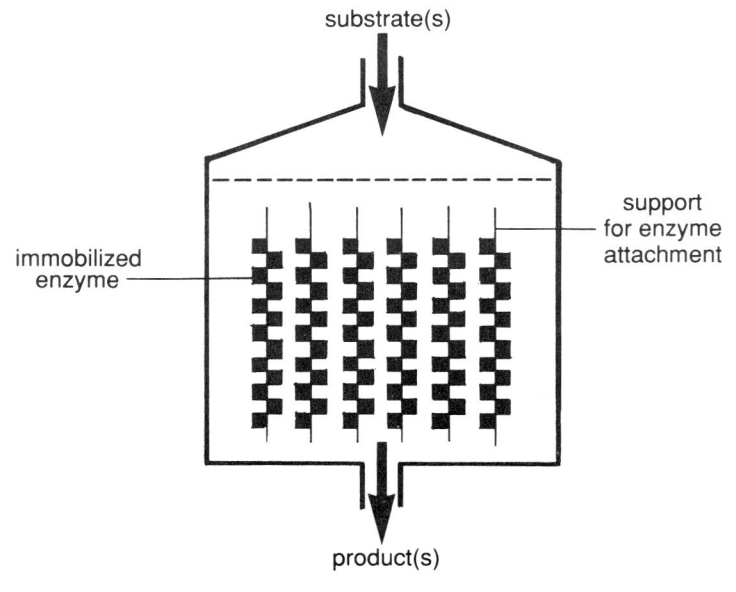

Using immobilized enzymes

Advantages of immobilized enzymes

a The enzyme can be re-used and so the cost of buying new enzyme is reduced.

b The products do not have to be separated from the enzymes.

c Waste disposal of used enzymes is not necessary. Factory effluent does not therefore cause so much pollution.

d They can be used in continuous systems. Normal soluble enzymes can only be used in batch systems.

e Industrial processes involving more than one enzyme can be set up and can run continuously.

DID YOU KNOW?

High-tech champagne

Makers of champagne may soon use yeast 'beads' to change ordinary wine into more expensive champagne. To make champagne, live yeast is added to bottled wine. Over a period of time, it ferments the sugar in the wine and releases bubbles of carbon dioxide. Each bottle, angled neck-down in special racks, must be turned by hand to make all the yeast in the bottle settle on the cork. When this happens, the bottle's neck is frozen, the bottle swiftly turned upright and the cork eased out. Pressure from the gas expels the frozen plug of yeast and the bottle is re-corked.

The new process, developed in France, uses yeast in capsules of gel. The 300-odd beads added to each bottle are far easier to extract than yeast cells. They quickly sink to the cork when the bottle is turned upside down, so champagne can be stored in any position, thereby saving space.

Hi-tech champagne

Now try these!

Which of the advantages of immobilized enzymes could be applied to the process described above?

Wonder Drugs and Wonder Microbes

The discovery of antibiotics

In 1928 Alexander Fleming was studying bacteria. He grew colonies of them on mixtures of food and **agar jelly** (made from a seaweed extract) in glass dishes called **Petri dishes**. (The Petri dish is named after its inventor, Julius Petri. He was the assistant to Robert Koch, often described at the father of microbiology.) The Petri dishes that Fleming was using became contaminated by a type of fungus. Fleming noticed that bacteria would not grow near the fungus. He identified the fungus as *Penicillium*. Some years later scientists proved that this fungus was making a chemical which stopped the growth of bacteria. They called the chemical an **antibiotic**. Today very many different antibiotics are used to help fight bacterial diseases. Some are made on vast scales by biotechnology.

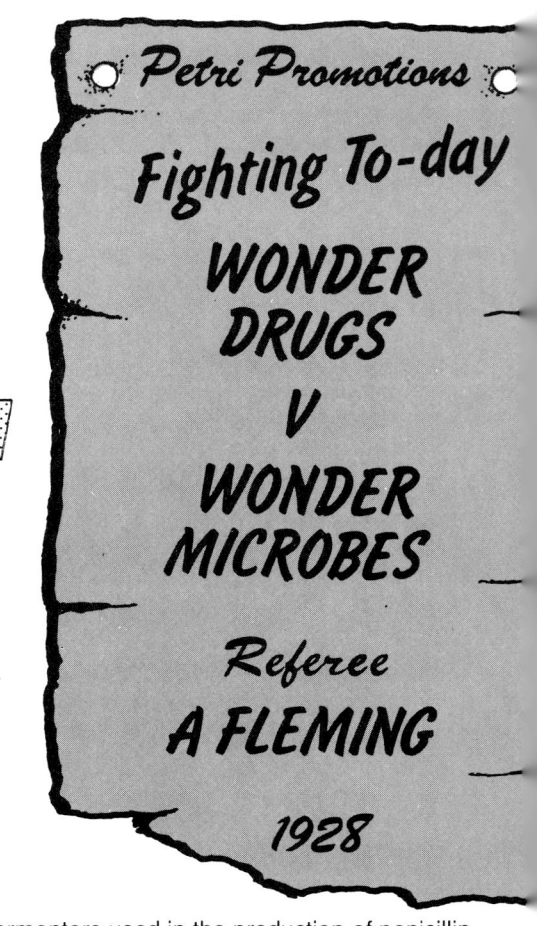

Petri Promotions

Fighting To-day

WONDER DRUGS

V

WONDER MICROBES

Referee

A FLEMING

1928

Fleming's Petri dish

One of the giant fermenters used in the production of penicillin

As long ago as 1939 mass production of the antibiotic made by *Penicillium* (**penicillin**) was attempted. The pioneers in this field were Howard Florey and Ernst Chain. The problem they faced was that the fungus uses up all its food and air as it grows. It produces waste products that build up and harm it. Biotechnologists designed production units which kept bringing new food and air while removing waste products. By 1943, penicillin was produced in 1000-gallon tanks. Many casualties in World War II owe their lives to penicillin which prevented bacterial infection of their wounds. Today new species of *Penicillium* have been found which can make 200 times more penicillin than the *Penicillium notatum* which contaminated Fleming's Petri dishes in 1928.